John Fyfe

ONE HUNDRED AND FIFTY YEARS
1846 - 1996

To: Sue
with best Wishes
Duncan
April 1996

BY APPOINTMENT TO HER MAJESTY THE QUEEN
SUPPLIERS OF QUARRY AND CONCRETE PRODUCTS

Foreword

As Managing Director of John Fyfe Limited I feel very privileged to be asked to write this foreword.

1996 is a very special year in our history. Firstly we are celebrating our 150th Anniversary (1846-1996) and secondly we pay tribute to the man, John Fyfe, who started it all.

As you will read in this commemorative book - John Fyfe was a man of immense stature. Humble of birth, he quite literally powered his way into the local history books. Acknowledged as being a benefactor to the City of Aberdeen he also enjoyed both national and international recognition.

Through sheer hard work, aided by an inventive mind and a keen eye for business, he laid the solid foundations of a company that has grown and prospered over the years with quarrying still very much its core activity.

In this book we honour the man and we honour the company.

I do hope that you will enjoy this book and in particular its wide and diverse collection of old photographs that portray the company's history, so eloquently.

John M Hume
Managing Director

Four Chief Executives

John M Fyfe (1906-1948)

Andrew Mutch (1948-1967)

John R Mutch (1967-1988)

John M Hume (1988-present)

Portrait of John Fyfe by John Singer Sargent
City of Aberdeen Art Gallery and Museums Collections

JOHN FYFE - THE GRANITE MASTER

John Fyfe was born at 'Goodhope' Bucksburn, in 1830, the eldest son of James Fyfe and Elizabeth Strachan. His father ran a quarrying business at Tyrebagger quarries, some six miles north-west of Aberdeen. Sixteen year old John inherited the business in 1846, on the death of his father.

In January 1868 he married Barbara Stevenson, daughter of the grocer in Dalmadilly, a hamlet close to the quarry at Kemnay. The house known as Fairview, was built for them beside the quarries and there they lived for several years before moving to Beechgrove House in Aberdeen. They had a family of eight daughters and two sons. John Malcolm Fyfe succeeded his father in the business. William died in 1911.

One of the daughters, Grace, suffered from rheumatoid arthritis. To try and alleviate her condition, she moved for a time to Egypt, hoping that the drier climate would be beneficial. There is, in existence, some correspondence from 1897 between Grace and her grandmother, Rachel Annand, describing the events on a cruise up the River Nile. Her father also writes describing the work involved in the building of the pyramids and how stones, some weighing as much as 65 tons, were shipped from the granite quarries 500 miles up river and then transported several miles across the desert to the building site.

Following the death of John Fyfe in July 1906, doctors advised that Grace should move to a milder climate. Beechgrove House was sold and the family moved to Surrey.

There are at present, two grandsons of John Fyfe who take a keen interest in the company. Graham Bower, son of Joan Amelia Fyfe and Haddon Anderson Bower, lives at Putney Heath, London, and Evers Austen, son of Florence Eva Fyfe and Rev Wilfred Austen, lives at Tenterden, Kent.

John Fyfe

Twenty miles or so north-west from the city of Aberdeen is Kemnay, a very pleasant, Aberdeenshire village which would be very much like any other village in the valley of the Don - but for one thing.

Long before planning authorities were ever heard of, its feudal superior insisted that the houses of the village be built from the beautiful hard material which was so easy to obtain, almost next door, along the Aquithie Road.

Thus, it differs from its neighbours. The fine village of Kemnay, draped in its sequinned garment of sparkling silvery grey, stands apart and is quite unique. Although Kemnay is an ancient settlement, it was, until the middle of the nineteenth century, a truly rural community. However, the development of its quarry changed it radically.

John Burnett, Laird of Kemnay, started extracting the beautiful grey granite, flecked with black, in the 1830s to provide building stone for the extensive renovations then being carried out at Kemnay House.

But it took the entrepreneurial skills of businessman, John Fyfe, to exploit the potential of the quarry in a really big way.

By the mid 1850s he was supplying stone from his quarries at Tyrebagger Hill for the bridges on the Alford Valley Railway. Adam Mitchell, a prominent Aberdeen builder, who was building bridges along the line, suggested to Mr Fyfe that stones could be quarried on the hill of Kemnay, thus cutting down on the cost of cartage. Following a visit to Kemnay, John Fyfe secured a lease from the laird for part of the workings on Paradise Hill.

Such then was the ability of the young John Fyfe, that, by the time he was 24 years of age he was sending out more granite from Aberdeenshire than any other man in that business.

Kemnay Quarries flourished. Men flocked to the new enterprise and soon Fyfe had to build tenements to house them as there were virtually no available properties in Kemnay. He erected four blocks in all. Two were built to the north of the quarry workings, beside the railway and were known as the High and Low Siding. The other two were built by the side of the old road from the village to Dalmadilly and were known as Paradise Cottages, or more familiarly, the Raw (Row). These properties were demolished in the 1960s, and the tenants rehoused in more modern houses in the village. The present concrete block making plant was then erected on the site.

Equipment was rather primitive at the time John Fyfe arrived in Kemnay and a face quarry was developed. The workings were driven in on the level as opposed to the pit system which was eventually developed.

Soon it was realised that better stone could be obtained by quarrying down, rather than into the hill. In the 1860s, in conjunction with Andrew Barclay, a young engineer from Kilmarnock, John Fyfe turned his mind to solving this problem and developed the Scotch Steam Derrick. This was first used at Kemnay and later introduced elsewhere. It was to revolutionise the entire quarrying industry.

On a trip up Deeside, John Fyfe saw an ingenious method used by a postman for carrying the mail across the river. This was achieved by means of a rope slung between two posts, one on either side of the river, with the mail hung from the rope and then pulled across.

Fyfe's inventive mind was soon at work and legend has it that he planned the construction while sitting in church, visualising the gallery and the pulpit as anchor points. The aerial ropeway was better known as the Blondin, named after the famed tight-rope walker who was 'at the height of his career' at the time. The Blondin transporter allowed quarrying to go deeper, in search of better quality stone.

Shortly after the quarries were opened at Kemnay, the Alford Valley Railway came into operation making the movement of stone to Aberdeen, and beyond, much easier.

John Fyfe was soon turning out top quality granite but there were still some sceptics - amongst them the Edinburgh architects, Peddie and Kinnear, employed to design the new Aberdeen Town House in the 1860s.

They had specified the use of sandstone in the mistaken belief that they could never obtain enough granite for the great block of buildings they visualised. Although their suggestion caused local uproar, the architects and Town Council refused to give way until John Fyfe guaranteed to supply every ton of stone required. Thus the Town House, with its magnificent clock tower and corner pepper-box turrets, completed in 1872, was built in Kemnay granite. In the years which followed, the same silvery stone was used to build the Fire Station in King Street; the Salvation Army Citadel in the Castlegate; The Caledonian Hotel; the new Post Office; the Northern Assurance Company offices; His Majesty's Theatre and buildings in Union Terrace, Aberdeen.

Many fine churches were also built in 'Kemnay' - Queens Cross and Beechgrove being two notable examples. Most spectacular of all was Marischal College, described by some as "a birthday cake in granite". It is the second largest granite building in the world, after the Escorial in Spain. Designed by A Marshall Mackenzie, Aberdeen, in a neo-gothic style of architecture, it was built by local builder, John Morgan, and officially opened by King Edward VII in 1906.

By the turn of the century, Kemnay's population had risen to 3,000 due not only to the opening of the quarry, but also to the introduction of the new railway.

As the years passed, John Fyfe opened other quarries in the area such as Tom's Forest, some two miles down the railway line towards Kintore, which had stone of a slightly darker hue than Kemnay. He also worked quarries at Corrennie and Tillyfourie, mid-way between Kemnay and Alford.

Corrennie granite is salmon-pink in colour with a grey fleck shining through and is one of the hardest granites in the country. Tillyfourie on the other hand is more of a grey-blue colour and was mainly used in the kerb and sett trade.

The passing years saw many changes in the quarrying industry but John Fyfe was always at the forefront, trying out new ideas and skills. He was the first quarryman to carry out blasting by electric detonation, thereby making the process more predictable and thus safer.

Huge quantities of granite were now being sent far afield to such contracts as the foundations of the Forth and Tay bridges; the Royal Insurance Company's head office at Brighton; the Liver Building in Liverpool and several London bridges including the Tower, Blackfriars, Southwark, Vauxhall, Kew and Putney. The Queen Victoria Memorial too, opposite Buckingham Palace, was built in sparkling light grey Kemnay granite.

Kemnay granite was also used on several projects along the east coast of the country in the construction of numerous harbours and breakwaters but the principal markets were to be found in London. Here large quantities of stone were supplied for the Thames Embankment and Fyfe's own vessels, the Black Dwarf and the White Witch, transported stone into the Thames Estuary over a seven year period. The building of the Thames Embankment alone kept 500 masons in constant work dressing stones to fill the two ships that steamed ceaselessly between Aberdeen and London.

John Fyfe was noted for his public-spirited generosity. Following the Dee ferry boat disaster of 1876 it seemed inevitable that an iron girder bridge would be built over the River Dee in Aberdeen. John Fyfe then submitted a price, thousands of pounds lower than any other, to ensure that such an important structure should be constructed in granite. The splendid Victoria Bridge was opened in 1881.

John Fyfe died in 1906 at the age of 76.

An "In Memoriam" in the *Aberdeen Free Press* said at the time:

"Aberdeen itself owes Mr Fyfe a lasting debt of gratitude, not only for the distinct lead he has consistently given in fostering the artistic development of architecture in granite work, but for his public-spirited generosity in making it possible on more than one occasion to retain inviolate the most striking aspect of Aberdeen as the Granite City".

His passing was a great blow to the granite industry in Aberdeen. Many large contracts had come to the city through his influence. For instance when the Glasgow Municipal Building for Design, to be built in granite from Argyllshire, was found to be too costly, the building committee consulted Mr Fyfe. He suggested that the basement, cornice and other principal areas might be produced in pink granite. The result was that a very large quantity of Fyfe's Corrennie granite was prepared and dressed in Aberdeen whereas the granite order was initially destined to have gone elsewhere.

Another example of his influence involved the construction of a breakwater at Sunderland. This was specified in concrete, from foundation to coping, until Mr Fyfe suggested to the committee, that by facing it with granite, the concrete would be protected from the action of the salt water, giving a much better long-term prospect. His recommendation was accepted and this provided a number of years work for "quite a gang of men".

Given this kind of experience, it was no wonder that Kemnay granite workers were in great demand. Many North East masons worked in America all summer, and came back to Kemnay when the inhospitable American winter made work impossible.

Legend has it that one man, James Bisset, went to Odessa, Russia in the 1860s, with his wife, to instruct the men there in the workings of granite. Being an ardent Scot, he took with him his fiddle and a copy of Robert Burns' works. But the democratic views expressed in Burns' poems were not appreciated by the Tsarist autocracy and Bisset was, in due course, deported. He made his way back on foot to Britain with his wife and two small children, earning a meagre living as he went by playing on his fiddle, reels and strathspeys learned in his childhood. For the rest of his life, his son, following in his father's footsteps as a quarryman at Kemnay, was known as 'The Rooshan'.

The years between 1906 and 1948 were years of consolidation for the company. John Fyfe's son, John M Fyfe, continued the good works set by his distinguished father. New buildings and structures such as the Cowdray Hall, the County Buildings, King George VI Bridge, Aberdeen Art Gallery and the Usher Hall in Edinburgh were all built in the company's granites. The granite yards at Blaikies Quay and Seaforth Road were kept busy in the supply of stone to residential, commercial and monumental contracts whilst Kemnay Quarries, as always, continued to produce vast quantities of granite setts for most of the major high streets of the country.

In 1941, a concrete brick press was installed at Kemnay. The basic raw material was granite dust, a by-product of the crushing plant installed around the turn of the century. The granite dust was until then considered to be of little or no use.

Mr John M Fyfe died in 1949 and was succeeded by Mr Andrew Mutch, a colleague director who had joined the business in 1928. Mr Mutch became the company's third Managing Director and latterly its Chairman. Under his direction the company continued to flourish.

With great vision, Andrew Mutch energetically developed the company's diversification into concrete products. He could foresee that the decline in demand for granite building blocks, after World War II, was going to create a crisis at Kemnay Quarries, so he set about looking for a more cost-effective substitute masonry material that would sit comfortably alongside the company's traditional materials.

In 1957, he introduced *Fyfestone*, a reconstructed stone split block which closely resembled natural stone. This product, manufactured at Kemnay, became an instant success and was widely specified throughout the United Kingdom. Today, the name *Fyfestone* is synonymous with reconstructed stone, everywhere.

Concrete bricks, too, were proving to be so popular that they had to be "rationed out" to local builders. By 1964, the annual sale of bricks exceeded 18,000,000.

At this time, kerb and paving sales were also running at a very high level and the company prospered to such an extent that in 1965 it "went public".

Andrew Mutch said at the time "We are going public because we have been extensively adding plant and growing particularly quickly over the past ten years. There comes a stage when a firm becomes just a bit too big to remain a private company".

In 1967, Mr Andrew Mutch had to retire due to ill-health. By this time he had built up an enviable reputation as a very astute and successful businessman, highly respected by his peers. He had successfully and skillfully guided the granite business through difficult years and established a thriving concrete product section to the business. Little perhaps did he realise what a legacy he had left as Fyfe concrete is now one of the largest concrete businesses in Scotland.

His son Mr John R Mutch took over as Managing Director at a particularly difficult time when Aberdeen Construction Group (ACG) was in the process of being formed.

Aberdeen Construction Group was a bringing together of John Fyfe Ltd, George W Bruce Ltd (Readymixed Concrete, Precast Concrete and Concrete Block Manafacturers), Alexander Hall and Son (Builders) Ltd, Lewis Middleton Ltd (Civil Engineers), W J Anderson Ltd (Civil Engineers and Precast Concrete Manufacturers) and William Tawse Ltd (Civil Engineers).

These companies represented the very cream of the city's building and civil engineering industry and it was a group formed to strengthen the positions of all its member companies at a time of strong, local economic growth.

An interesting aspect of ACG's growth over the years is that it was not a smooth uninterrupted upward path. There were years when the figures reflected distinct pauses, sometimes set-backs, before the growth trend was resumed.

In character with the companies who had come together to form the group, ACG extended its activities throughout the UK from Shetland to Southampton accepting exposure to the vicissitudes of the national economy which this entailed.

Under the guiding hand of John Mutch, the company over the next twenty years moved steadily forward. In 1987 Aberdeen Construction Group was acquired by Raine plc and six months later in 1988, John Fyfe Ltd was sold on to Evered plc.

At this point, Mr John R Mutch retired and Mr John M Hume became its new Managing Director and Chief Executive.

The company then accelerated forward faster than anything previously experienced in its long and distinguished history. Massive capital injections allowed the company to re-equip with modern plant; to purchase new trucks and thereby expand its transport fleet; to acquire competitor companies and set up fresh green-field sites right across the densely populated and more lucrative markets of Central Scotland.

In 1991, Evered merged with the international quarrying company, Bardon. Bardon's chief executive, Mr Peter W. G. Tom, recognised the development potential of John Fyfe and encouraged its continued expansion. He also agreed that the old and respected quarrying name of John Fyfe should continue to represent Bardon's building materials operations in Scotland.

John Fyfe has now twenty three quarries and gravel pits; eight coated stone plants; twenty four ready mixed concrete depots; eleven concrete product plants; three road surfacing depots; a natural stone division including thirteen memorial centres - all based in Scotland. The company also has a quarrying, ready mixed concrete, concrete product and road surfacing operation based at Newport, Isle of Wight.

By 1996, more than £5,000,000 will have been invested in Fyfe's Duntilland Quarry in Strathclyde on the M8 mid-way between Glasgow and Edinburgh. This "mega quarry" is at the heart of a massive new Scottish roads programme and it is geographically situated to service both road and commercial contracts in all of Central Scotland. Duntilland's core product "crushed stone" is not only a high quality product in its own right but it is also the basic raw material used at the quarry to produce "value added" products such as coated stone, concrete products and ready mixed concrete at John Fyfe's Central Scotland Depots.

The company has also dramatically increased its spread of ready mixed concrete sites throughout the country and is now, in this its 150th anniversary year, Scotland's largest supplier of concrete.

Natural Stone has also continued to feature high in the Fyfe portfolio. The recently formed Bardon Fyfe Natural Stone company not only markets its own granites but also imports stone from other parts of the world. Natural stone is very much in demand as a specialist "up-market" and prestigious building material.

Locally quarried and imported stone has been recently used in several high-profile office developments in Glasgow; the new Department of Social Security offices in Leeds; London's Bishopsgate and several other major contracts in the City of London. Only a few years ago more than 4,000 tonnes of Kemnay granite was used in the building of the Bon-Accord Shopping Centre in Aberdeen.

At a time when traditional skills are in decline, John Fyfe is still a major employer of craftsmen in the production of architectural stone, monuments and memorials. Today, the modern John Fyfe operation has a spread of over eighty outlets. There are depots ranging from 15-20 people, close to big centres of population like Dundee down to one man operations in the Highlands.

Despite the UK's construction industry being in deep recession, during 1994 and 1995, John Fyfe Limited has fared far better than most.

Chief Executive, Mr John M Hume acknowledges and pays tribute to the company's outstanding history which is based on the ideals and principles of a man who possessed shrewdness, business foresight and a dogged perseverance whereby "he took occasion by the hand" and skillfully developed his undertakings with an energy and determination which were bound in the end to bring their own and due reward.

Kemnay Quarries 1879, photographed by George Washington Wilson. Clearly seen in the upper left is the head mast of the Blondin, first erected at Kemnay in 1873. By this means granite could be readily lifted from the floor of the quarry. It is recorded that one day 'trucks were run alongside the principal quarry and 40 tons of dressed stone were raised from a depth of 200 feet. The stones were placed into trucks, which were then run down into the railway siding - all in the short space of an hour and three quarters'. (*Free Press*, 12th May 1883). A steam derrick crane can be seen on the floor of the quarry. This machine which was first introduced at Kemnay went on to revolutionise quarrying.

City of Aberdeen Art Gallery and Museums Collections

Ropeway at Abergeldie Castle, Deeside circa 1870s. Legend has it that it was this ropeway, designed to carry mail across the River Dee, which inspired John Fyfe to design the Blondin and thus revolutionise the extraction of stone from deep quarries.

City of Aberdeen Art Gallery and Museums Collections

Head mast of the Blondin at Kemnay 1879. By means of this device, stone could be lifted from the floor of the quarry and set down on the quarry rim, or loaded into bogies which could then be moved round the workings on the network of railway lines. This was particularly important when it was found that the best stone came from relatively deep beds.

City of Aberdeen Art Gallery and Museums Collections

A scene early in the life of the quarry showing opened-fronted sheds which were built to enable masons to dress stones free from the vagaries of the weather. The roofs of these sheds opened to allow the travelling steam crane to deposit the stone into a suitable working position for the mason. John Fyfe is the figure in coat and top hat on the right of the photograph.

John Fyfe Ltd.

A Blondin was constructed at a later date that could lift stone from the floor of the quarry and deposit it within easy reach of the travelling cranes.

City of Aberdeen Art Gallery and Museums Collections

Such was the demand for granite in the second half of the nineteenth century that quarries were opened up over a large part of Aberdeenshire. Picture shows early work at Tillyfourie Quarry (1879), six miles south east of Alford. Clearly seen in this photograph is an early example of a pneumatic rock drill. Until the introduction of this technology all holes were drilled by hand, a slow laborious process. This quarry became the principal centre of the kerb and sett trade.

John Fyfe Ltd.

Workers at Tillyfourie Quarry showing off their new steam travelling crane acquired from Thomas Smith, Engineers, Rodley near Leeds in 1901.

John Fyfe Ltd.

One of the most prestigious buildings in nineteenth century Union Street, Aberdeen, was the Town House erected 1866 - 1872. The decision by Edinburgh architects Peddie and Kinnear to build it in sandstone caused great consternation amongst the City Fathers. However, John Fyfe personally guaranteed to supply every ton of granite from his quarries at Kemnay to the site - and the specification was changed.

City of Aberdeen Art Gallery and Museums Collections

Aberdeen Art Gallery, designed by A Marshall Mackenzie. This is a fine example of how granite from two of John Fyfe's quarries could be used to give contrast and harmony in a building. The upper portion of the gallery is in the silver stone from Kemnay contrasted with Corrennie salmon pink granite below.

City of Aberdeen Art Gallery and Museums Collections

In the 1920s tenemented properties in Blackfriars Street, Aberdeen, were demolished and the Cowdray Hall and War Memorial were erected to plans by A Marshall Mackenzie and Son and built of Kemnay and Corrennie granite. Also cut from Kemnay stone is the large carved lion which now forms the central feature of the memorial's facade.

City of Aberdeen Art Gallery and Museums Collections

The extension to Marischal College built in the closing years of the nineteenth century by John Morgan to designs by A Marshall Mackenzie, was opened by King Edward VII in 1906. It has been described by some as a 'poem in stone'. Next to the Escorial in Spain, it is the largest granite building in the world. This neo-gothic extravagance in Kemnay granite illustrates what could be achieved architecturally using the then recently introduced pneumatic cutting tools. It is probably the most imposing use of Kemnay stone anywhere in the world.

City of Aberdeen Art Gallery and Museums Collections

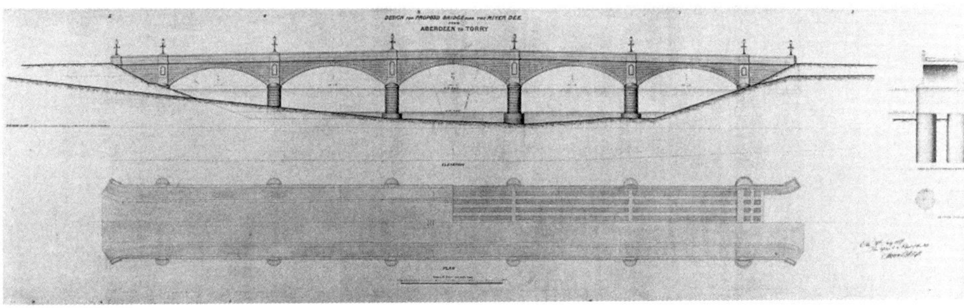

Following the disastrous sinking of the ferry, crossing the River Dee to Torry in 1876, when 32 lives were lost, it was decided to erect a bridge to span the river. Mr Fyfe's offer to construct a granite bridge at a cheaper cost than any of the alternative schemes was accepted and the five arch Victoria Bridge then became the link between Torry and Aberdeen in 1881.

City of Aberdeen Art Gallery and Museums Collections

Ballater Bridge. Designed by Messrs Jenkins and Marr, architects and engineers, Aberdeen. The bridge was built by John Fyfe, Kemnay and opened by Queen Victoria on 6th November 1885.

City of Aberdeen Art Gallery and Museums Collections

John Fyfe built four blocks of houses for incoming workers to Kemnay Quarries. Pictured here is the High Siding which housed seven families. The annexe at the end nearest the camera was a small grocer's shop.

Duncan Downie

'*The smith a mighty man was he.*' A group of blacksmiths and associated workers taken outside the smiddy door at Kemnay Quarries at the turn of the century.

City of Aberdeen Art Gallery and Museums Collections

A group of quarry workers around the turn of the century. The age range varies greatly from nipper to old man. They encompassed a wide range of trades - such as borer, fireman, cutter, mason, settmaker and blacksmith.

Duncan Downie

The use of steam as a motive power was utilised from an early stage. This view shows an early model of a travelling crane which was used to move stones around the masons' yard. A network of railway lines was laid along the top of the spoil heaps and hand-bogies were used to move both stones and waste material.

Duncan Downie

This view of the blacksmiths' shop at Kemnay gives some idea of the variety of 'goods' which were made here. In the foreground is a heap of chains for the blondin boxes, whilst a variety of hammers, puncheons and drills can be seen lying around.

Duncan Downie

The following four illustrations were taken in June 1939 by the British Geological Survey. Electricity came to Kemnay around 1936 and within the next three years steam was displaced by electricity. The boiler houses disappeared and new Blondins were also installed. The large steel crane can be seen on the rim of the quarry, and to the left may be seen the embarkation point of the 'hutches', the means by which the men were lowered to the floor of the quarry. A number of settmakers' scathies can be seen lined out along the top of the waste tips. The blondin mast at the right of the picture is situated at what was known as the 'spion kop', named after a battle in Natal during the Boer War. (The name spion kop is derived from the Dutch language, meaning a "look-out hill").

Director, British Geological Survey

View looking back towards the 'big hole' from the spion kop with the blondin lifting cable in the middle of the picture. A large stock of cassies or setts can be seen with the rail network weaving off to the right of the picture, crossing the bridge across the access road up the hill. To the extreme left is the 'howler' or 'number two quarry'.

Director, British Geological Survey

View looking back across the railway bridge towards the masons' sheds. Settmakers' scathies are in the foreground and behind is a blondin mast.

Director, British Geological Survey

View showing the travelling steam crane operating in front of the masons' sheds. Several of the roof sections can be seen opened. Above the sheds there is a blondin house perched on the side of the quarry, whilst beyond is 'number two quarry'.

Director, British Geological Survey

Following the downturn in the use of granite during the 1930s, part of the masons' sheds was used for the manufacture of concrete products including kerbing, fence posts, slabs etc. This view shows the stockyard, with the electric power house beside the sheds.

Director, British Geological Survey

Jock Daun, stonecutter. The stonecutter reduced the granite blocks, following blasting, to a more manageable size. These were then dressed by the stone masons.

Duncan Downie

Settmakers at Kemnay Quarries in the 1930s. Left to right: Bill Harvey, Bruce Reid, Bill Stuart, Douglas Lawrie.

Duncan Downie

George Ewen, Senior, settmaker. Like many others of his generation, George travelled to America in the 1890s. There he worked making setts for the Oakland Bridge, San Francisco before returning to Scotland. He spent the rest of his working life at Kemnay Quarries.

Duncan Downie

After forty years of quarrying, the accumulation of spoil was considerable. John Fyfe installed crushing equipment at Kemnay Quarries to recycle this waste material. The reclaimed aggregate was then used for ballast on the railways, sub-base for road making, and raw material for the construction industry. Illustrated here is a group of quarry workers beside the crushing plant.

Duncan Downie

William Henderson, settmaker. Apart from a brief time in America around 1905, he spent most of his working life at Kemnay Quarries. He was one of the few remaining settmakers still employed in the 1950s.

John Fyfe Ltd.

Granite from Kemnay has been used for many different contracts throughout the world. Part of the block featured here was used for the Lord Inchcape Memorial which was erected at Glen App, Ballantrae, Ayrshire in 1936.

Duncan Downie

In 1941, a brickmaking plant was installed at Kemnay. This plant utilised the large stock of granite dust which had accumulated over the years from the crushing plant. The bricks are made on Alexander presses and hand stacked onto pallets before their transfer to the drying sheds. Because the bricks require 'gentle handling' the tendency has been to employ female labour over the years. In the course of a day some 30,000 bricks are manufactured. Pictured from left to right: Margo McGillivray, Jenny Adams and Annie Taylor.

John Fyfe Ltd.

Since 1941 various concrete products have been produced at Kemnay. 1957 was the year that *Fyfestone* was introduced. Large concrete blocks are made and then cured for a month before being split by guillotine. This process produces a face closely resembling that of naturally quarried stone. *Fyfestone* still remains popular with all sectors of the building and civil engineering industry. It has four finishes - split, pitch-faced, weathered and bullnosed.

John Fyfe Ltd.

For many years quarry products were moved by rail. During the 1920s and 30s, with the advent of motorised transport, more materials were moved by road. Pictured here are 8 ton blocks of granite being loaded onto a J. G. Barrack lorry. Five of these large blocks were taken to Aberdeen to be carved into ornamental lions for the new King George VI Bridge over the River Dee. With the outbreak of war, these were never used.

John Fyfe Ltd.

Much of the loading was initially by hand. This picture shows cassies being loaded on to a lorry. James Gibb (Curly) is in the centre of the picture with Jock Daun to the right.

Duncan Downie

After manufacture, the bricks were built onto pallets and then hand-loaded onto lorries. When they reached site they had to be hand-offloaded as there were no forklifts or mechanical offloading systems at that time.

John Fyfe Ltd.

Handling methods continued to improve and here we see a pallet of common bricks being emptied into a tipping lorry from a fork lift truck. The bricks were then tipped on site.

John Fyfe Ltd.

Featured here is Curly Gibb at the controls of the Blondin. There are two drums in operation. One operated the travelling rope which moved the cradle across the hole whilst the other operated the lifting rope.

Aberdeen Journals Ltd.

One of Kemnay Quarry's finest moments! In September 1956, one of the biggest stones ever seen at Kemnay was blasted from the face. The measurements of the stone were 50ft x 25ft x 10 to 17ft and it was estimated to weigh at least 1,000 tons. Stone from this massive rock was used in the construction of the former C & A building at the corner of Union Street and Bridge Street, Aberdeen. It was also used to build Telephone House, Dundee and for the widening of the Bridge of Don, Aberdeen. The stone was shot from halfway up the quarry and it slid 200 feet down the face, landing in one piece at the bottom. The figures on the stone are Robbie Thomson, Bill Law (Hoop) and James Clark (Shochey).

Aberdeen Journals Ltd.

This illustration shows the concrete products stock yard at Fledmyre, Forfar (1994). Here a fully modernised plant produces bricks, paving blocks, kerbs and slabs. Because of its centralised location, Fledmyre is able to service outlets throughout Tayside and the rest of the country.

John Fyfe Ltd.

Tom's Forest Granite Quarry, Kintore (1995). A quarry of high activity, which not only services the 'outside market', but provides a 'down stream' supply to the company of all sizes and gradings of quarried stone, sand and gravel for the production of coated stone and concrete.

John Fyfe Ltd.

Duntilland Quarry, Salsburgh, Shotts (1996) close by the M8, midway between Glasgow and Edinburgh. In 1995 phase 1 was completed and by 1996 £5,000,000 will have been invested to make this quarry one of the largest and most modern of its kind in Scotland. Its annual output is in the region of 1,000,000 tonnes of quarried stone with a capacity to produce even more. Total reserves at the quarry are estimated to be in the region of 100,000,000 tonnes.

John Fyfe Ltd.

Fyfe Roadstone is the surfacing division of John Fyfe. This division has laid many miles of motorway and highway surfaces throughout the country with coated stone from the company's coating plants. During 1995 Fyfe Roadstone surfaced the Skye Road Bridge which links the island to the mainland.

John Fyfe Ltd.

The Big Bang! (1989). Blasting is a regular occurrence at Tom's Forest Quarry - where most of the material is crushed and graded to provide aggregates for the company's concrete products, coated stone and ready mixed concrete activities. Crushed granite is also used for road construction, filter media, ballast etc.

John Fyfe Ltd.

The impressive new coated stone complex at Duntilland Quarry, Shotts (1996) alongside the M8. Here a fast turn round of lorries, conveying top quality-assured coated stone deliveries, throughout Central Scotland, has elevated Duntilland to the forefront of the Scottish coated stone market.

John Fyfe Ltd.

At Westhill Granite Works, Aberdeen, this 3 metre primary Sideral circular saw, which is one of several, cuts 10mm down into the stone at every pass.

John Fyfe Ltd.

In 1989-90 four Barsanti frame saws were installed at Westhill Granite Works at a cost of £1.5 million. These multi-bladed saws are capable of producing 140 architectural cladding slabs from a 15 tonne granite block.

John Fyfe Ltd.

The skills of the stone mason are still very much alive. Although much of the stone-cutting and shaping is now achieved by computerised machinery, stone masons continue to pass on their unique engraving and hand polishing skills.

John Fyfe Ltd.

Craftsman at work hand polishing specially made granite units. There is still no substitute for such skills.

John Fyfe Ltd.

There are OMAG block making machines located at Dyce and Kemnay. These fully automated plants have a combined daily production capacity of 50,000 concrete blocks. Here a revolving brush removes any residue from the top surface of the blocks.

John Fyfe Ltd.

In 1941 the first concrete brick press was installed at Kemnay. The bricks were removed from the press by hand. Today (1996) the brick presses (above), at Fledmyre, Forfar are automated and quality-assurance systems are in place.

John Fyfe Ltd.

The boys in blue! A 1980s group photograph taken at the old smiddy, Kemnay Quarries. With the emergence of Health and Safety, protective clothing and hard hats are in evidence.

John Fyfe Ltd.

1996 - The modern face of John Fyfe Ltd. The smart new corporate identity encapsulates the efficiency and capability of this concrete truck mixer. John Fyfe is one of the largest suppliers of ready mixed concrete in Scotland, and has a geographical spread of twenty four depots.

John Fyfe Ltd.

1996. John Fyfe's most recent acquisition. This concrete product factory, located in Airdrie, manufactures hydaulically pressed kerbs, paving slabs, edgings and a unique range of reproduced stone decorative pavings and kerbs.

John Fyfe Ltd.

1994. The new Denburn inner ring road in Aberdeen. Natural granite, quarry products, ready mixed concrete, coated stone and concrete products were all supplied by John Fyfe Ltd.

John Fyfe Ltd.

The Last Word

Cartoon No 30: Northern Figaro

After John Fyfe's death, the following verse was penned by one of his staff.

'Epitaph on the Granite King'

Here lies the bones of Mr Fyfe
A pushing hero all his life
A worthy, wise, and good man here
Could well adorn a higher sphere;
And when his soul went up the hill
His busy mind was active still
He sold in Heaven, before an hour,
Ten thousand tons of four by four
And wanting to encourage trade
He wired to Moir* to have them made.

* William Moir was a manager at Kemnay Quarry at the time of John Fyfe's death.

ACKNOWLEDGEMENTS

The Board of Directors of John Fyfe Limited wish to thank the following for providing research material which has enabled the production of this book.

Aberdeen Art Gallery and Museums
Aberdeen City Archivist
Aberdeen Journals Ltd
Aberdeen Public Library
Aberdeen University Library Special Collections
National Library of Scotland
North East Scotland Library Services
Petroleum Association
The Director, British Geological Survey

All families and friends who have supplied photographic material and assisted in identifying former quarry employees, and in some instances providing the tales behind the picture.

The company also record their thanks to:

Mike Dey, Moira Gemmill, Lyn Harman and Deirdre Grant from Aberdeen Art Gallery for their help with research, typesetting and layout of the publication.

Duncan A Downie, Kemnay, researcher, for the use of his archive and the benefit of his wise counsel.

And latterly to Sandy Argo, our Head of Marketing, John Fyfe Ltd, for his unstinted effort and hard work in co-ordinating the whole venture.

Printed by Gilcomston Litho (Aberdeen) Ltd.